FOUR CENTURIES OF MUSIC IN IRELAND

The Trinity College Harp. Late medieval period, fifteenth century. For a full description, see Treasures of Early Irish Art (*Metropolitan Museum of Art, New York 1977*) *and J. Rimmer,* The Irish Harp (*Dublin 1969*).

FOUR CENTURIES OF MUSIC IN IRELAND

Essays based on a series of programmes broadcast to mark the 50th anniversary of the BBC in Northern Ireland.

Edited by Brian Boydell

BRITISH BROADCASTING CORPORATION

Published by the
British Broadcasting Corporation
35 Marylebone High Street
London WIM 4AA

ISBN 0 563 17760 8

First published 1979

Typeset in Great Britain by
Eta Services (Typesetters) Ltd., Beccles, Suffolk

Printed in England by Whitstable Litho Ltd., Whitstable, Kent

Contents

List of Illustrations

The illustration on the cover is reproduced from *O'Farrell's Collection of National Irish Music for the Union Pipes,* published *c.* 1800. (National Library of Ireland)

Foreword

This booklet is based on a series of programmes broadcast in 1974 by the BBC in Northern Ireland to mark the completion of fifty years of broadcasting in the province.

Professor Boydell, who edited the original series, has modified the plan of the scripts to make the information more suitable for reading as distinct from broadcasting, and to bring it up to date.

Although a short booklet such as this cannot attempt to provide anything like a comprehensive survey of four centuries of music in Ireland, we hope that it will prove of use and of interest to students as well as to general readers in an area in which reliable information is notably hard to come by.

I would like to thank Mr Robert Pugh, Head of Administration, BBC Northern Ireland, for special assistance in publishing the booklet.

Edgar Boucher

Introduction

In 1974, to mark the occasion of fifty years of broadcasting from Belfast, I devised in association with the BBC a series of thirteen musical programmes with associated talks, presenting a survey of Irish musical life during the past four centuries. This booklet is an attempt to bring together in as compact a form as possible the chief facets of Irish musical life during this period which were presented in these programmes. The approximate timespan of four centuries is imposed by the almost complete lack of any precise evidence concerning the nature of music performed or produced in Ireland before the end of the sixteenth century. We do know from literary and pictorial evidence that music played an extremely important part in the social life of medieval Ireland: what was clearly a polyphonic choir was established in St Patrick's Cathedral in Dublin in 1431; and we know that harps such as the famous fourteenth-century one in Trinity College were played by musicians who enjoyed a very high position in the social hierarchy. A few fragments survive from the cathedral music, but no trace remains of the music of the Gaelic civilisation, which was so enthusiastically described (albeit in rather vague terms) by Giraldus Cambrensis after his tour of Ireland in the twelfth century.

There is of course no lack of surmise, mainly of a romantically fanciful nature, concerning the nature of the music which was played and composed in medieval Ireland. The tragedy is that no documentary evidence survives from earlier than the end of the sixteenth century, apart from the internationally inspired church music. The main reason for this is that early Irish music was an aural tradition, and no record has yet been found in the form of written notation. The other reason, which is possibly important in connection with monastic and cathedral music, is that the turmoil and warfare which so seldom left this unfortunate country at peace for very long, was hardly conducive to the preservation of manuscripts.

The strife which destroyed so much of the tangible evidence of the country's musical past was a symptom of the sharp division between the native Gaelic community and the colonial ruling society, each with its separate culture insulated from the other by strong political and religious barriers. The former is expressed in the justly famous folk heritage, which (bearing in mind the warning about wild surmise) could well contain traces of a lost medieval tradition; while the latter is a reflection with local colouring of the mainstream of European music, most notably celebrated in Handel's visit to Dublin for the first performance of his *Messiah* in 1742.

In the chapters which follow, we are not just concerned with Irish music, or music composed in Ireland, but with the various kinds of music which were both made and played in Irish communities. The distinctively Irish songs and dances of the folk tradition, and the music of the Irish harpers, are described by Seán O Boyle and Gráinne Yeats; and this aspect is balanced by articles treating of the music enjoyed by the Anglo-Irish ruling classes, as typified by the numerous concerts which added so significantly to the richness of cultural life in the eighteenth century, and the enthusiastic development of amateur music and the fervour for opera in the nineteenth century, described by Professor Fleischmann and Dr Walsh. All this activity founded a heritage which laid the foundation for contemporary musical life in Ireland, when changed conditions made possible a remarkable upsurge of creative activity, as described by Colman Pearce who, as staff conductor of the Radio Telefis Eireann Symphony Orchestra, has a widely representative and intimate knowledge of contemporary Irish music. Church and organ music, which reflects an important aspect of social life, is described by the eminent organist Gerard Gillen, who is a lecturer in University College Dublin; and the equally important reverse of the coin, the contemporary styles of local popular music, have their advocate in David Hammond. Finally, Professor Anthony Hughes of University College Dublin assesses the present scene with an eye on the future.

Inevitably the limitations imposed by a short booklet have meant the exclusion of several more specialist aspects of Irish musical life which were included in the original series of broadcasts; but reference to the selected bibliography and list of recordings should help to fill in the gaps left after reading what cannot claim to be more than a series of vignettes describing four centuries of musical activity in Ireland.

Brian Boydell

The Making of Irish Traditional Music
Seán O Boyle

One summer evening about twenty years ago when I was collect-
ing songs in the mountains of Tyrone I happened to call into a
house in Derrynanaugh (Doire na nEach), near Altmore. It was
early in the evening and I should have known that most of the
family would be down in the fields at the hay. They were. But
there was one little girl about fourteen years of age in charge of the
place (Margaret Loughran was her name) and, cheerfully enough,
she told me she would sing for me – a wee bit of a song she had
learned from her granny.

It was on the twen - ty ___ fourth of June ___ As I sat

weav - ing up - on my loom ___ I heard a thrush sing-in' in a

bush and the song she sang was 'A Jug of Punch' Lad-ly fol da

dee, Lad - ly fol da dee di did-dle um, Dee id-le doo id-dle

Dee di did-dle um Lad - ly fol da dee di did-dle um,

Dee - dle id - le dee - dle ad - dly Dee di dum

That was all she had of it, she said. But it was quite clear from Margaret's accent and style of singing and even from the content of the song itself that the song was part of her own environment.

It is an Irish traditional song. In its music it is modal. Through an accident of history it is in the English language, but in its words it echoes faintly the prosody of the older Gaelic tradition – notice the assonantal rhyming of 'June' and 'loom', 'bush' and 'Punch'.

We find more than an echo of Gaelic prosody in many other Irish songs in the English language. We find direct imitation, as for instance in this snippet from an Ulster song:

> It's light and airy I've tramped through Derry
> And to Portaferry in the County Down
> But in all my rakings and undertakings
> I met no equal to Sweet Omagh Town.

In its verse structure that song belongs to a centuries-old Gaelic measure (Ochtfhoclach) which you may perhaps recognise in the modern Irish 'Preab san Ól':

> Is iomaí slí sin a bíos ag daoine
> Ag cruinniu píosaí's ag deanamh stair
> 'S a laghad a smaoineas ar ghiorra an tsaoil seo
> Go mbeidh siad sínte faoi leac go foill.

If you wish you may sing 'Sweet Omagh Town' to the tune of 'Preab san Ól', for Irish tunes are intimately connected with the Gaelic metres which shaped them originally and, conversely, with the metres derived from them by folk-poets. 'I always make my poems to the lie of a good tune,' said an Armagh woman to me some time ago.

Come to think of it, that is what Thomas Moore did when he wrote English words to the Irish airs collected by Bunting and Petrie. In the process he enriched English literature with many new poetic metres including the metre known in Irish as *amhránaíocht*. This metre is basic to some of our most characteristic vocal melodies and when grappling with one of these Moore wrote this line:

At the mid-hour of night when stars are weeping I fly

If he had known the Irish language, if the sound of Gaelic metres had been ringing in his ears, he would have placed internal rhymes in a line something like this:

At the mid-hour of night by the light of the stars I fly

Of course not all English-language songs in our tradition show signs of Gaelic prosody. Indeed many of the songs now sung traditionally are not even of Irish origin. Ever since the Battle of Kinsale (1601) there has been a constant interchange of songs between Ireland and England. Military establishments in various parts of the country constituted the original link, then came the Plantations and intermarriage and in later years the migrations of labourers to England and Scotland. All these influences have left us Scottish and English songs in every county: Barbara Allen, Lord Randall, Will you go, lassie go?, Edward, The Ploughboy, The Bleacher lassie, The Bonny Bunch of Roses O!

But though it is undoubtedly true that two important tributaries, Scottish and English, flow into the mainstream of Irish song, it is most important to remember that the Irish language is the *fons et origo* of that mainstream.

And now, a word about the music itself. It is based not only on the metres and rhythms of Gaelic poetry but also on the scales within the compass of the harp, which from early medieval times until the end of the eighteenth century was regarded above all others as the musical instrument of the Irish.

The Irish harp once it was tuned was fixed in pitch. The harpers' scales were therefore based on the only system possible on their instrument and that was the modal system.

The scales (unfortunately still called 'modes') are six in number and their character is determined simply by the way their tones and semitones are disposed in them. It is convenient to think of them in two sets of three, involving a minimum change of pitch:

1 Doh mode CDEFGABC′
2 Ray mode DEFGABC′D′
3 Me mode EFGABC′D′E′
4 Fah mode CDEF♯GABC′
5 Soh mode DEF♯GABC′D′
6 Lah mode EF♯GABC′D′E′

Margaret Loughran's little song is in the Soh mode. You will see – and I hope hear – the Soh mode in its entirety above the words 'Ladly fol da dee di diddle um' in her lilting chorus.

Lilting is of course generally associated with dancing, but then, song and dance go together in Ireland and many of our song patterns are actually derived from dance rhythms. Poets set their words to jigs in 6/8 time, to slip jigs in 9/8 time and to reels in 2/4 and 4/4 time. Eoghan Rua Ó Súilleabhan earned himself the

Paddy Tunney, from Belleek, one of the most respected singers in Ireland. Among his many other talents are lilting, dancing and storytelling. He has recorded extensively.

title of Gaelic Ireland's greatest metrist by writing in involved metres to the tunes of what we now call Set Dances.

The dances which survive in the living tradition are – the jig, the reel, the hornpipe and some comparatively recent polkas and barndances. The reel is of Scottish origin, no one knows the origin of the hornpipe, and the provenance of the double jig, which must be the oldest of Irish dances, is still a matter of controversy. However it must be said that the vast majority of our dance tunes are of Irish origin, even those tunes still used the polkas and barndances.

At the present time we Irish people seem to be more interested in the instrumental tradition than in our heritage of song. This is a pity because the singing tradition is the weak link in the musical chain that unites us with our past. It has already suffered from the almost complete disappearance of the Irish language as a vernacular and from the effects of social change in the life-style of the people. It remains to be seen whether or not its dissemination by radio and television, by record player and cassette, will keep it alive as well and as surely as oral transmission has kept it for centuries.

Irish Harp Music

Gráinne Yeats

'Of all countries in the world, Ireland possesses the most beautiful and varied folk music', wrote Sir Arnold Bax. Irish folk music
is, indeed, very beautiful, and of an astonishing variety: two
qualities that derive from centuries during which the varied
strands of the Irish tradition were woven together to create the
remarkable music that we know today.

In any country there tends to be a division in the musical scene.
On the one hand, there is the art music composed by the musician
trained to that end, and performed by trained professional
musicians. On the other hand, there is folk music in all its vocal
and instrumental manifestations, the music that is not composed
by anybody in particular, but grows out of the natural occupa-
tions and inclinations of the ordinary people. In Ireland, however, this normal division was complicated by the existence, set
between art music and folk music, of a third musical tradition:
this was the music of the harpers, the true art music of the Gaelic
nation.

In Gaelic Ireland the harpers were the professional performers,
granted a high status in society, as the musicians of the aristocracy.
Music was always very important to the Irish, and the harp in
particular is referred to over and over again in Irish myths, and
in manuscripts. It is clear that even in very early days, the harpers
occupied an important place in the estimation of the people. From
at least the eleventh century, the harpers had acquired a position
of high esteem. They were expertly trained court musicians,
attached to the retinues of kings and chiefs, writing music to

Denis Hempson (1695–1807), the last known player to use the old traditional technique of playing with long fingernails, played at the Belfast Harp Festival in 1792.

Patrick Quin, harper to the Irish Harp Society. Reproduced from the Syllabus *of the first commemoration of Carolan which took place under the auspices of the Irish Harp Society in the Private Theatre in Fishamble Street, Dublin, on 27 September 1809.*

order, and trained in a strict discipline about which, however, we know little. We do know that the harp was used to accompany the recitation of epic poetry, and it seems likely that there were also solo pieces and songs, but this must remain a matter of conjecture. The harping tradition was an oral one, passed by ear from player to player, and never written down.

So long as the great Gaelic houses continued to flourish, power, music and poetry maintained their happy relationship. However, increasing pressure was put on the Gaelic order from outside invaders, so that by the year 1600 or so the old order was well on the way to collapse. When disintegration finally came, both poets and harpers found themselves without patrons. For some, privilege remained, for they secured positions as harpers to the new landed gentry, the Anglo-Irish, who now replaced the old Gaelic chiefs. This opened up the harpers' music to new influences. Where, formerly, they had worked happily in a Gaelic idiom to please Gaelic chieftains, now they had to please new masters whose tastes were very different. It was the music of London, and of the European continent, that interested these new masters, though in the course of years they developed an interest in Irish music also.

Other harpers became travelling musicians, going from house to house, and making music for any who would pay them or grant them hospitality. This led to a cross-fertilisation in musical styles, a twofold exchange of traditions. Where formerly the harpers had been concerned with formal, stylised music, now they associated with folk musicians, and heard music of a different kind. They adapted their music to what they now heard, while at the same time giving their own airs to the folk musicians.

From the seventeenth century onwards, the harp declined steadily, both as to the numbers playing it, and to standards of music and performance. By the end of the eighteenth century the tradition had almost ended, and the last recorded traditional player died in the middle of the nineteenth century. As the tradition of the harpers was purely oral, we might know little or nothing of their music, were it not for an event that took place in 1792. This was the Belfast Harp Festival, the last occasion on which the

The Assembly Rooms in Belfast, scene of the first Harp Festival in July 1792. The building is now the premises of the Northern Bank Limited. (Ulster Museum)

harpers came together to play. This festival holds an important place in Irish musical history, for it marked the first and the last time that the music of the harpers was written down in any quantity.

The festival was organised by some prominent Belfast citizens, who were interested in the traditional harp and who hoped to promote enthusiasm for the instrument. They offered attractive fees to induce harpers to come and play for a number of prizes but, despite this, only ten Irish players came, plus one Welshman. The once numerous band of harpers was by now obviously pitiably small. For three days, these musicians played through their repertoire of Irish music, while Edward Bunting, a young organist from Armagh, went amongst them and took down their tunes. After the festival was over, he visited some of the harpers at their homes, taking down more music from them, and learning from them details of their playing techniques and their traditions.

In addition to his work with the harpers, Bunting collected music also from many folk musicians, and he published sections of this extensive collection in three volumes, over a period of some fifty years. The Bunting Collection was the first really extensive publication of Irish traditional music, and it illustrates very well its beauty and variety, as well as the coming together of the various styles that can be traced throughout the music. This collection is a source of endless pleasure and fascination for anyone interested in the roots of Irish music.

Here there are to be found simple folk tunes in plenty, along with the lively, rhythmical music written to be played for dancing by pipes or fiddle. Alongside these are a host of elegant and sophisticated melodies, obviously written by trained musicians. There are many instrumental pieces with obvious harp thumb-prints, even though their origins are unknown. Some of these have variations in the manner of the eighteenth century, yet with distinctive Irish twists. There are strange unmelodic pieces that seem unmusical to present-day ears, and sound like some voice from the past. Are these the remnants of the ancient music once used to accompany poetry? There are just a few pieces and songs attributed to named harpers, as well as many written by Turlough Carolan (1670–1738). His music is easily recognised, for he wrote in a very distinctive style, much influenced by such composers as Corelli and Vivaldi, whom he greatly admired.

It is clear that the harpers played a vital role in the make-up of Irish traditional music. Originally the art musicians of the Gaelic nation, in their later role as itinerant musicians they formed a bridge between folk and art music, while still clinging to their own inherited discipline. Long after the passing of the old traditional harpers, their influence is still evident today. Many of the great songs, the love songs in particular, can only have been written by highly skilled musicians. They are elaborate and sophisticated composed songs, in a style quite different from the simpler productions of folk musicians. It is surely this amalgam of folk, harp and art traditions that has created in Ireland a body of folk music that is amongst the most beautiful and varied in the world.

Church Music in Dublin, *1500–1900*
Gerard Gillen

Although Irish monks are known to have composed some of the finest of Gregorian chant melodies, the vicissitudes of Irish history prevented the same development of the creative art here as characterised monastic life in continental Europe and Great Britain. First there were the Norse invasions from the eighth to the eleventh century, which were particularly directed against the monasteries; then the Norman conquest from the twelfth to the fourteenth, the chaotic state of religious organisation in the fifteenth, and the confiscation and closure of the monasteries in the sixteenth century. However, the musical establishment of Dublin's two ancient cathedrals, Christ Church and St Patrick's, largely managed to survive the religious and political turmoil of the centuries.

The musical traditions of St Patrick's began in 1432 when Archbishop Talbot founded a choir school which flourishes to this day as the Cathedral Grammar and Choir School. The first reference to an organ in St Patrick's was Archbishop Tregury's gift of a 'pair of organs' in 1471 for use in the Lady Chapel, and the first organist of whom there is record is one William Herbit who was appointed in 1509. The first professional organist of Christ Church Cathedral was Robert Hayward, 'a singing man', to whom the Dean and Chapter in 1546 awarded an annual stipend for life of £6.13s.4d, twelve pecks of wheat and eight pecks of malt, 'a livery coat, a cartload of wood at Christmas, and the chamber by the east of the churchyard'. His duties were carefully set forth: he was to play the organ, 'to keep Our Lady's Mass and anthem daily, Jesus' Mass every Friday', etc. Of the actual music performed in the Cathedrals at this time we know very little, although it is known that the Sarum Rite was still adhered to, and the masses of Taverner, Aston and Robert Fairfax were in use.

John Farmer and Thomas Bateson, organists of Christ Church Cathedral from 1595 to 1599 and 1608 to 1630 respectively, were the first of a number of distinguished English musicians who came as organists to one or both of Dublin's Cathedrals. Their coming suggests that Dublin cathedral music must have had a high reputation in England. Bateson, best known for his madrigals, came to Christ Church from Chester Cathedral, and we may assume that his seven-part anthem, *Holy Lord God Almighty*, was added to the Christ Church repertoire. Benjamin Rogers, a chorister of St George's Chapel, Windsor, was organist at Christ Church from 1639 to 1646 before returning to Windsor. As a composer he established a type of Short Service which was emulated by such eighteenth-century composers as Kent, Nares and Ebdon.

Having held cathedral positions in Gloucester, Winchester and Salisbury, Daniel Roseingrave, reputed to be a pupil of Purcell and Blow, came to Dublin and held both Cathedral posts simultaneously from 1698 to 1727. He was succeeded in both positions by his second son, Ralph, who held the posts until his death in 1747. Both Roseingraves composed anthems, services and organ voluntaries, and were responsible for introducing the music of the Restoration composers to Dublin's cathedrals. John Clarke, later known as Clarke-Whitfeld, a pupil of Oxford's Professor of Music, Philip Hayes, came to Dublin to hold both cathedral positions briefly in 1793. He proceeded north to Armagh in 1794 and returned to England after the 1798 rising and eventually became organist of Gloucester Cathedral in 1820. He was a voluminous composer, very popular in the first half of the nineteenth century. Of his services, that in E major is probably the best, and of his anthems, *Behold how good and joyful* and *In Jewry is God known*, stand up reasonably well to critical examination.

There were, of course, many notable native holders of these cathedral offices, some of whom were very versatile musicians.

Cork-born Philip Cogan, for example, was organist of St Patrick's from 1780 to 1806, but is more remembered today as the teacher of Michael Kelly and Thomas Moore and as a pianist, than as a church musician. Yet he composed some very accomplished anthems and organ voluntaries which followed the standard English genre of the period. During the tenure of the historically obscure John Matthews who was organist of St Patrick's from 1806 to 1827, McGregor's *Pictures of Dublin* claimed that Dublin could boast of the finest cathedral choir in the British Empire, and in 1815, the *Freeman's Journal* proudly wrote of the 'excellence of the music and singing' at St Patrick's, and commended the 'solemn and impressive manner in which this imposing service is presently performed'. Mention must also be made of the famous Sir John Stevenson who was vicar-choral of both Christ Church and St Patrick's where his tenure largely coincided with that of Cogan. His music occurs frequently in the service lists of both cathedrals right through the nineteenth century, though its quality hardly justifies the Dean of St Patrick's description of him as the 'Irish Handel'.[1]

The latter part of the nineteenth century was dominated by the presiding presence in both cathedrals of Sir Robert Prescott Stewart. He had a facile pen and composed prolifically services and anthems in a style that can fittingly be described as English Cathedral Victorian. His *Concert Fantasia* for organ and a few other pieces deserve rehabilitation. His main historical importance probably lies in the fact that he was the early teacher of Charles Villiers Stanford (1852–1924) before the latter's departure to Cambridge as organ scholar of Queen's College. It is a little ironic that Stanford and his close contemporary, Armagh-born Charles Wood, are two Irish composers who achieved the widest international appreciation for their Anglican church music. They brought back something of the spirit of Purcell to English service music and strengthened its formal shape by transferring to it something of symphonic procedures.

For historical reasons music in Roman Catholic churches was

[1] *The Freeman's Journal*, 8 January 1823.

rather less developed, and it was not until the 1780s, in consequence of Lord North's Relief Bill, that the Catholic Liturgy could be freely celebrated with its full adornments. In April 1789 Giordani composed a *Te Deum* which was sung at the conclusion of High Mass in the Archepiscopal Chapel in Francis Street, Dublin, to celebrate the recovery to health of King George III. Dublin's first professional Catholic organist was Edinburgh-born Haydn Corri (of Italian family), who was appointed to the newly opened Pro-Cathedral in 1827, where the performance of one of Mozart's masses was described in the *Freeman's Journal* as having produced an 'extraordinary effect',[1] a comment not without ambiguity of meaning! Corri's appointment was the first of a number of foreign appointments to Irish Catholic churches, a trend which continued well into the present century. In Cork from 1878 to 1889 there was Leopold de Prins; in Dublin, Alois Volkmer (St Andrew's, Westland Row), Alessandro Cellini (Carmelite Church, Whitefriar Street) as well as other more native organists such as John Glynn (Dominick Street), Joseph Goodman (St Peter's, Phibsboro'), and J. J. Johnson (St Catherine's, Meath Street), all of whom were enthusiastic composers and were imbued with what were known as 'Cecilian' ideals.

The Cecilian movement originated with the Ratisbon/Regensburg group of composers, liturgists, and scholars – Witt, F. X. Haberl (editor of the monumental Palestrina complete edition), Haller, Mitterer and Stehle – who sought to purify Catholic church music of Italian operatic and secular influences, and to effect a return to what was considered to be the ideal liturgical music: plainsong and Palestrina. In Ireland the Cecilian ideals were promulgated by the monthly *Lyra Ecclesiastica* which began publication in October 1878. Its pages show remarkable zeal and enthusiasm on the part of its contributors, and erring churches were quickly and severely admonished as the following extract illustrates: 'We have heard with great regret that the latest addition to the repertoire of the choir of the Church of the Three Patrons, Rathgar, is an adaptation of "chi mi frena" from

[1] 4 January 1830.

Donizetti's Lucia di Lammermoor . . . it is a satisfaction to know that, thanks to the initiative of his Grace, the Archbishop, the recurrence of such scandal will be rendered impossible before long.'[1] Pope Pius X's famous *motu proprio* of 1903 on church music can thus be seen as the final formulation of a whole century of international attempts to establish a fitting ecclesiastical style, and in Dublin this led directly to the formation of the Pro-Cathedral's Palestrina Choir in the same year. This, coupled with the fact that in 1886, Maynooth College, the National Seminary for the training of priests, had secured as its first Professor of Music, Father Heinrich Bewerunge, a German musician of remarkable talent and scholarship, ensured that Roman Catholic church music was committed to the plainsong and polyphonic revival as the twentieth century began.

[1] *Lyra Ecclesiastica,* June 1879, p. 78.

Music in Eighteenth-Century Dublin
Brian Boydell

In comparison with its previous history, the city of Dublin settled down in the eighteenth century to a period in which the elegance and idle affluence associated with a colonial governing class formed the ideal background for the cultivation of the arts which were considered to be an essential decoration of sophisticated and cultured life. Dublin, as the second city to London in the British Isles, entered upon what is usually thought of as its 'golden age', in which a highly cultivated society encouraged and patronised the arts, including most notably architecture, literature, the theatre and music. This fashionable sophistication, reflecting that of London, soon spread to the larger provincial cities; notably Cork, Limerick and Waterford. Except for a few isolated events, such as performances of Arne's *Comus* in 1788 and 1793, and the important occasion of the first Harp Festival in 1792, Belfast hardly figures on the musical map until the nineteenth century, when a remarkably rapid growth of musical activity promoted largely by the enthusiasm of Edward Bunting, the folksong collector, found fertile soil for development in the expanding community.

The importance of such glorious events as Handel's visit to Dublin, culminating in the first performance of his *Messiah* in 1742, has often led to an assumption that the period was crowded with performances of similar quality. That there was an astonishing amount of musical activity, and that a great number of distinguished European musicians came to Ireland and contributed to this activity is without question. What is not so often realised is that, with certain notable exceptions, the quality of the music that was presented and what can be deduced concerning the standard of performance does not bear favourable comparison when viewed in the European context.

Other factors should also be borne in mind when assessing the Irish musical scene in the eighteenth century – factors which are so obvious that they are often overlooked. In spite of Dublin's reputation as a centre for the arts second only to London in these islands, it consisted of a relatively small isolated population geographically situated on the western rim of Europe where it could not enjoy the benefits of musicians passing through on their way to and from other great musical centres. Furthermore, as a capital, it was not a focus for the life of the country. The split between Gaelic and Anglo-Irish, and between Catholic and Protestant was more completely marked than ever before. Such events as the publication in c. 1742 and 1746 of sets of variations on *Eileen a roon*, the use by such composers as Shield and Giordani of Irish tunes in comic operas, and the publication of the melodies of Carolan the harper-composer represent little more than a veneer of local flavour upon what was essentially a reflection of the London taste for European music.

During the course of the eighteenth century the fashion for attending musical performances and theatrical presentations in which music played an important part spread from being a comparatively restricted activity closely connected with the court society of Dublin Castle to one which involved a wide section of the community. Dublin soon attracted musicians of European fame, such as Geminiani, Dubourg, Michael Arne and Tommaso Giordani, who made it their home. Handel, T. A. Arne, Pasquali, Castrucci, J. F. Lampe, Pinto, Tenducci and many others paid extended visits to the city. The remarkable extent of musical activity in the middle of the eighteenth century can be deduced from events advertised in the 1749–50 season, which reveal a total of nearly three dozen performances of 16 oratorios, 59 of operas or musical plays, and a wide range of instrumental music by Corelli, Vivaldi, Handel, Geminiani etc.

A SUMMARY OF THE MORE IMPORTANT MUSICAL ITEMS
PERFORMED IN DUBLIN DURING THE 1749–50 SEASON

Oratorios and Choral Works

Bononcini	*Funeral Anthem*		2	perfs.
Boyce	*Solomon*		2	,,
Dubourg	*Birthday Ode*		1	,,
Handel	*Acis and Galatea*		7	,,
Handel	*Alexander's Feast*		4	,,
Handel	*Deborah*		2	,,
Handel	*Esther*		3	,,
Handel	*Joshua*	('Never done here before')	3	,,
Handel	*Jubilate and Anthems*		1	,,
Handel	*Judas Maccabeus*		1	,,
Handel	*Messiah*		2	,,
Handel	*Samson*		1	,,
Lampe	*Birthday Ode*		1	,,
Pasquali	*Noah*	(First perf.)	1	,,
Pergolesi	*Stabat Mater*		4	,,
Purcell	*Grand Te Deum*		1	,,
		Total	36	,,

Operas and Musical Plays

A total of about 56 performances of 17 different items put on at the Smock Alley and Aungier Street theatres, including:

at least 4	performances of	*The Beggar's Opera*
4	,,	Thomas Arne's *Comus*
8	,,	Purcell's *King Arthur*

Instrumental Music

Corelli	Considerably more than 7 performances of 6 different concertos
Geminiani	More than 4 performances of 3 different concertos

Handel	*Fireworks Music:* 4 performances
	Overtures to: *Acis and Galatea, Esther, Scipio, Rodelinda* and *Pastor Fido*
	Concerto No. 5
Mudge	Concerto No. 1
	Trumpet concerto ('a new favourite concerto')
Pasquali	Frequent performances of A Grand Concerto Piano e Forte for the violin
Thos. Roseingrave	Organ concerto
Vivaldi	More than 6 performances of 5 different concertos

Unattributed concertos: French Horn, Trumpet, Organ, etc.

During the first quarter of the century the Theatre Royal in Smock Alley (opened in 1661) was the only building which could hold an audience of any size apart from the cathedrals and larger churches, and Dublin Castle. The Smock Alley theatre met rivalry first from the Aungier Street theatre, which was opened in 1734 and offered a more capacious stage. It fell into disuse, largely due to poor acoustics, about 1750. Rivalry then passed mainly to Crow Street which was rebuilt as a theatre in 1758, having been a concert hall since it was erected at the request of the Musical Academy for the practice of Italian Musick in 1731. The Crow Street theatre closed in 1820 when stage music became the monopoly of the Theatre Royal in Hawkins Street (burned down in 1880).

The chief venues for oratorio and concert performances were firstly the Crow Street Musick Hall (1731–57) and Mr Neale's Great Musick Hall in Fishamble Street, which was opened just before Handel arrived in the autumn of 1741, and accommodated 700 people (without swords or skirt-hoops) for the first performance of *Messiah* on 13 April 1742. With the building of the Rotunda in 1764, the popularity of Mr Neale's Hall gradually declined, and it was turned into a theatre in 1777.

Apart from the commercial theatres, music in eighteenth-

DUBLIN
1756

Map showing the chief venues for
musical performances in Dublin in
the mid-eighteenth century.
(Drawn from Rocque's map of
1756 by Brian Boydell)

Crazy Crow, the Dublin instrument porter. James Caulfield, in
his Portraits, Memoirs, and
Characters of Remarkable
Persons (London 1819–20), includes a description of Crazy
Crow, whose real name was
George Hendrick. He was fined
and imprisoned in 1742 for having
stolen corpses from St Andrew's
churchyard. In 1762 he dropped
dead in Swan Alley.

FISHAMBLE STREET. DUBLIN. 1797.

Fishamble Street Music Hall, Dublin, 1797. Built by Richard Cassels in 1741, 'Mr. Neale's Great Hall' was opened on 2 October in time for Handel's visit to Dublin. The first performance of Messiah *took place here on 13 April 1742. With the building of the Rotunda in 1764 it was used less and less, and at the time of this illustration it was run as a private theatre. It was eventually sold to Kennan & Sons whose ironworks is still housed within the main structural walls.*

OVERLEAF *Advertisement from the* Dublin Courant *of 16 to 19 January 1747–8 inserted by George Brown, the instrument-maker of Crane Lane. With its amusing reference to Cane Flutes, this advertisement indicates the wide popularity of the German or transverse flute in Dublin at the time.*

GEORGE BROWN Musical Instrument Maker, dwelling at Mr, Hyens's, Cutler in Crane-lane, Dublin. has by his Skill and Industry, brought that Instrument call'd the German Flute to that Degree of Perfection, that the most Knowing in that Art can find no Defect in them, and by a new Machine of his own Invention, Gentlemen may with the greatest Facility found all the Notes of the said Instrument, from the highest to the lowest. He also makes excellent German Cane Flutes, for the Accommodation of those Gentlemen that wou'd recreate themselves abroad, and as he has been for this considerable Time past a successful Practitioner in his Art, and has wrought for the most eminent Masters in his Travels through Germany, Holland, Flanders and England, humbly hopes, Gentlemen, such as have occasion for said Instrument will favour him with their Custom, and they may be assured of getting as good Instruments from him as is possible to be made.

century Dublin was mainly promoted by numerous charitable musical societies which displayed a confusing inconsistency of nomenclature. Chief among them were Mercer's Hospital (which organised an annual benefit concert), the Charitable Musical Society for the Relief of Imprisoned Debtors (variously named) and the Charitable Infirmary (now Jervis Street hospital), all three of which benefited from the first performance of Handel's *Messiah*. In the second half of the century Lord Mornington's Musical Academy (1757–77) and the Irish Musical Fund Society (founded in 1787) were notably active; the former epitomising the aristocratic leadership of amateur musical activity with its titled membership and the statute which stated that 'No public mercenary performer, professor or teacher of music shall ever be admitted into any rank of the Academy on any account whatsoever'.

OPPOSITE *Graph showing the activity of the Dublin music trade up to 1850. The numerical totals of traders in printed music and in the instrument trade reflect the extent of musical activity. Further research will be necessary to produce a confident interpretation of the remarkable peak in 1820–25 followed by a dramatic fall in the number of traders. (From an unpublished study of the Irish music trade by Brian Boydell)*

The Dublin Music Trade 1650~1850

Numerical Totals of Music Traders in 5-year periods.

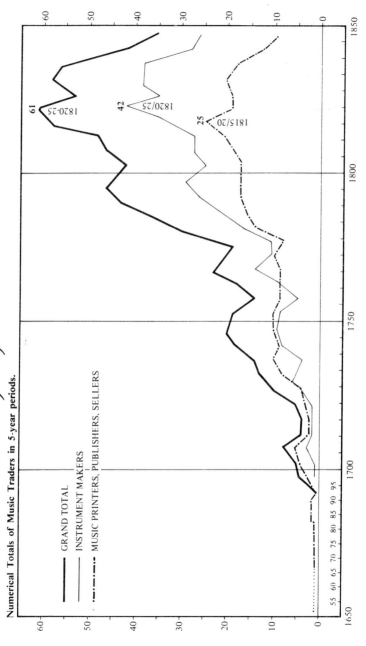

GRAND TOTAL

INSTRUMENT MAKERS

MUSIC PRINTERS, PUBLISHERS, SELLERS

The Earl of Mornington (1735–1781). Garrett Colley Wesley succeeded his father as Baron in 1758. He was the father of the Duke of Wellington. He became the first Professor of Music in Trinity College, Dublin, in 1764, obtaining his degree of Mus.D. in the same year. He founded the Musical Academy for Amateurs in 1757, was a noted violin and keyboard player, and was the composer of many partsongs and a well-known Anglican chant. (From the Duke of Wellington's collection)

The more important musical occasions in eighteenth-century Dublin consisted of oratorio performances in aid of some 'Great and Noble Charity', and theatre music, which varied from plays with extensive incidental music to full-scale opera. The audience, motivated by edification and social duty, approached oratorio with grave attention; whereas the theatre provided lighter entertainment. The fashion for Ballad Operas, beginning with Gay's *Beggar's Opera* in 1728, led to English comic opera; and Italian opera was brought to Dublin in 1761. Of the other types of concerts, the most common was a mixed 'Concert of Vocal and Instrumental Musick', usually promoted as a benefit for a professional musician. A great attraction at such concerts was to offer some unusual item such as '. . . this being the first time that (musical) glasses were ever introduced in concert' (Pockrich, 1743) or '. . . a young Miss, being the first time of her performance in public.' Outdoor concerts were very popular during the summer months, being held in such places as Marlborough Bowling Green, and the Gardens in Great Britain Street (from the proceeds of which Dr Mosse built the Rotunda Hospital). Amateur chamber music was encouraged as a social asset, and the demand for music and instruments supported an active music trade. The German (or transverse) flute became so popular from the 1720s on that in 1748, George Brown of Crane Lane was advertising that 'He also makes excellent German Cane Flutes for the accommodation of those Gentlemen that would recreate themselves abroad . . .'

As in England, the public looked mainly to foreigners for their music, but the active patronage of the nobility and gentry led to a certain amount of creative activity on the part of local composers such as the Roseingrave family – Daniel (c. 1650–1727), Ralph (c. 1695–1747) and Thomas (1691–1766) – and the Earl of Mornington (1735–81) who was appointed to the newly created chair of music in the University of Dublin in 1764. Francis Hutcheson (1721–80), who was Professor of Chemistry at the same university, wrote partsongs of considerable merit under the pseudonym of Francis Ireland. In February 1792 John Field first appeared in public and published his first known compositions. Also active at the close of the century were Philip Cogan (1748–1833) and John Stevenson (1762–1833) who provided accom-

The Rotunda and Round Rooms, Dublin, in 1795. Built by John Ensor in 1764 to hold an audience of 2000, the Rotunda usurped the role of the Fishamble Street hall as Dublin's chief concert hall. At the present time it is used as a cinema. (After a print by James Malton in the National Library of Ireland)

paniments for Thomas Moore's *Irish Melodies*.

With the passing of the Act of Union of 1800, and the abolition of the Irish Parliament, Dublin music lost much of its wealthy patronage. A tradition had however been established, and although opportunities for professionals decreased with the coming of a new era of amateur music-making, there was still sufficient activity to maintain 19 publishers and music sellers and 42 instrument makers during the period 1820–25.

Music in Nineteenth-Century Ireland

Aloys Fleischmann

Ireland in the nineteenth century was hardly a fruitful field for the talented or ambitious musician. Towards the end of the previous century there had been an upsurge of amateur activity under aristocratic patronage, and a small group of minor composers – the Earl of Mornington, Philip Cogan, Timothy Geary – had their glees, canzonets, harpsichord sonatas or suites published in Dublin or London, while music shops, instrument makers and music teachers flourished. The Act of Union in 1800 did not immediately affect the situation, but the gradual decline of Dublin as a social centre and the drift to London of the Anglo-Irish aristocracy and landed gentry led to a corresponding decline in patronage and in public interest. Had it not been for the Union, Dublin might well have become one of the liveliest capitals in Europe in its support of music and the arts. Instead, the annals record a long list of creative musicians who left to seek their fortunes in England or abroad, from John Field, Michael Balfe, Vincent Wallace and Charles Osborne to Charles Stanford and Hamilton Harty.

In the early years of the century music-making in Ireland was still dominated by the nobility and by the wealthier members of the community. To compensate for the decreasing amount of 'house-music', an effort was made to organise large-scale public concerts in Dublin with the founding of The Sons of Handel in 1810 by Francis Robinson for the provision of choral music, and of the Philharmonic Society for orchestral music in 1826. Francis Robinson's son Joseph initiated the Antient Concerts Society in

1834, which gave four or five performances each season. With his three brothers, Joseph Robinson was responsible for many of the leading musical events in the capital for the next fifty years. In 1843 the Society bought and later reconstructed rooms in Gt Brunswick Street known as 'The Antient Concert Rooms', which rapidly became the hub of musical activity in Dublin. A similar hall, the Music Hall in May Street, had been built by the Belfast Anacreontic Society in 1840 – a society founded in 1814 to sponsor an orchestra composed of professional and business men; while the Antient Concerts Society of Cork, founded in 1846 on the Dublin and Belfast models, ran a series of concerts annually in various halls. The concerts in all three centres were confined to members of their respective societies and their friends, and were fashionable events, with evening dress usually specified in the advertisements.

Towards the middle of the century the merchant and middle classes began to take the lead in amateur activity, and in 1851 John William Glover, organist of the Catholic Pro-Cathedral in Dublin, founded the Royal Choral Institute 'to establish in this country a large body of choristers composed chiefly of the working classes, capable of performing the best classical works, the performance of which is at present exclusively confined to private societies'. Glover was also Professor of Vocal Music in the Normal Training-School of the Irish National Board of Education, an appointment which marked the first step in the official recognition of music as part of the educational system, music being considered as having a moral and refining effect on children, and as a 'powerful instrument in softening their dispositions'. A similar viewpoint was expressed by the *Belfast Newsletter* in 1859 in connection with the opening of the Ulster Hall, since the smaller size of the existing Music Hall required prices of admission to be extravagantly high, so that people of modest means and the working classes 'were virtually excluded from every entertainment which would improve or elevate their moral and intellectual character'. Despite such sentiments, instrumental training had remained in the hands of private teachers, until in 1848 the Irish Academy of Music was founded 'for the purpose of establishing a school of instrumental music in the city of Dublin, the lack of which has been a great obstacle to the performance of first-class instrumental works for orchestra of the Dublin societies'. The Academy was reorganised in 1856, and the title 'Royal' added in 1872. A considerable time was to elapse before this headline was followed elsewhere – in Cork in 1878, when the Cork School of Music became the first municipally endowed school of music in these islands, and in Belfast when three different schools of music were launched between 1891 and 1899, though all three proved to be ephemeral.

Of all forms of music, opera throughout the century had the largest following. The Theatre Royal in Dublin had been opened in 1821, with a seating capacity of 3800, and Italian opera seasons with internationally famous singers were held several times annually, as well as in the Queen's Royal Theatre, opened in 1844. Operas produced in London or on the continent arrived in Dublin after a remarkably short time-lag, and some 150 different operas were staged in Dublin between 1850 and 1900, most of them unknown or little known in so far as the public was concerned. Touring companies combined a Dublin visit with visits to Belfast and Cork. In the 1860s light opera was the rage all over Europe, and the Gaiety Theatre was opened in Dublin in 1871 to cater for such operettas as those of Offenbach, Lecocq and Planquette, and, from 1876, of Gilbert and Sullivan presented by the D'Oyly Carte Company. Opera performances in Belfast's Theatre Royal were somewhat less frequent than in Dublin, and because of protests against their frivolity, there was a delayed reaction to the boom in operettas.

A noteworthy feature of each music season was the activity of the British military bands, which up to 1856 had been paid for by the officers out of their private incomes, and which were hired out for civic events. Members of the bands were constantly used to augment the amateur orchestras, both in the cities and the provinces. After 1856 the organisation of the bands was taken over by the War Office, yet the majority of the bandmasters were still foreigners, chiefly Germans. Civilian bands also flourished in large numbers, taking an active part in the temperance

Sir Robert Prescott Stewart (1825–94). Organist of Christ Church Cathedral in Dublin from 1844 until his death, and of St Patrick's Cathedral from 1852 to 1861, he succeeded John Smith as Professor of Music in the University of Dublin. He was conductor of the Dublin Philharmonic Orchestra from 1873, and the composer of cantatas, glees, songs and organ music. (From a portrait in the possession of the University of Dublin Choral Society)

crusades pioneered by Father Theobald Mathew from 1838. According as the Temperance Society spread, bands were to be found in almost every town from the middle of the century onwards.

In the cities one musician, as a rule, occupied a central position and dominated the scene. In Dublin from 1834 it was Joseph Robinson and his Antient Concerts Society, and later, Sir Robert Prescott Stewart, the Organist of St Patrick's, who succeeced Dr John Smith as Professor of Music at Trinity College, and also succeeded Dr Smith in his other appointments, with such resounding titles as Chief Composer of the State Music, Master of the King's Band of State Musicians in Ireland, and Composer to the Chapel Royal, Dublin. In Belfast the most eminent musician in the 1860s was Dr Edmund Chipp, who gave organ recitals and conducted major choral and orchestral concerts, while in Cork about the same time Dr J. C. Marks, organist of St Fin Barre's Cathedral, was able to mount a choir and orchestra of about 300 with his City and County of Cork Choral and Festival Society.

Despite all this activity, composition in Ireland was at a low ebb. The church music of Dr John Smith had a certain vogue, while the prolific Sir Robert Stewart wrote glees, odes and cantatas as well as church music, and edited the Irish Church

Hymnal. J. W. Glover produced a much-performed oratorio, *St Patrick at Tara* (1870) and an opera based on Goldsmith's *The Deserted Village* (1880). But the general impression of the work of all three is one of dullness and pedantry. Later in the century Dr James C. Culwick wrote a number of church services, part songs and some church music, Dr T. R. J. Jozé's choral arrangements of Irish airs were widely sung, and Percy French produced popular songs in a racy humorous style. But it was nearly the turn of the century before any music of quality emerged which could be identified as Irish, with Stanford's *Irish Symphony* (1887), his opera *Shamus O'Brien*, the cantata *Phadraig Crohoore* (1896) and the first of the Irish Rhapsodies (1901). Though Stanford lived in London, fathered a whole generation of British composers, and was himself steeped in the tradition of Schumann and Brahms, he remained conscious of his Irish roots, and some of his most successful works are those in which he makes use of the idiom of Irish folk song, or which have an Irish background.

Paradoxically, the advent of the Irish idiom into the field of orchestral music came at a time when the tradition itself was at its nadir. All through the second half of the century the music of the countryside had been suffering a continuing decline. Many of the best singers, pipers and fiddlers either fell victims to the famine of 1845 and the following years, or joined in the mass emigration to the USA. With the abandonment of the Irish language, the songs which had been the mainstay of the tradition gradually ceased to be understood except by the dwindling few still conversant with the language. At the start of the century Moore's *Irish Melodies* had made many of the traditional airs world-famous, but at a cost – for the original robust, racy or imaginative Irish verse he had substituted English lyrics which appealed to the polite conventions of the Regency bourgeoisie. So from Moore's time there were two streams – the one of songs and ballads with English words, the other of 'sean-nós' singing, in the old traditional style. According as the traditional music, both vocal and instrumental, waned, interest in it began to grow, and an increasing number of collectors commenced to work for its preservation, including Forde, Hudson, Pigott, Goodman,

Levey and Petrie. The Young Ireland movement had given rise to popular patriotic songs in the English language, while in the north Orange ballads, sturdier and less romantic than the ballads of the south, showed a vitality in defence of the Orange tradition as intense as the rebel songs of the nationalists.

Political activity and the movement for the restoration of the language towards the end of the century helped to stimulate support for the new awareness of the value of traditional music. In 1888 P. W. Joyce had published his *Irish Music and Songs* – the first collection to contain words in the Irish language associated with the tunes. In 1897 the Feis Ceoil was founded by Dr A. W. Patterson, and in the same year An tOireachtas was founded by the Gaelic League. The music section of the Oireachtas confined itself to the performance of Irish music, and to competitions for the arranging of folk song and for original music by Irish composers, while the Feis Ceoil became a general music festival on the lines of the English competitive festival, gradually spreading to centres all over the country.

At this time foreign musicians were still at the helm in the cities, namely Michele Esposito in Dublin, appointed Professor of Piano at the Royal Irish Academy of Music in 1882, who founded and directed the Dublin Orchestral Society from 1899, and in Belfast Adolf Beyschlag, who conducted the concerts of the Belfast Philharmonic Society from 1880, and was succeeded in 1887 by Francis Koeller. At the Belfast Feis Ceoil held in 1900 the prize winners included Carl Hardebeck and Hamilton Harty, names which were to figure largely during the coming years. The turn of the century, however, can be seen as the dividing line between an era in which activities in the cities were largely directed by foreign musicians, and traditional music declined disastrously, and our own century, in which the emigration of talent has largely ceased, traditional music has been revived, and a generation of Irish composers have begun to speak with a voice of their own.

Opera in Nineteenth-Century Dublin

T. J. Walsh

The light of other days is faded
And all their glories past
For grief with heavy wing hath shaded
The hopes too bright to last

These sentimental lines were written by Alfred Burn for an air in Michael William Balfe's opera, *The Maid of Artois*. It was an *andante cantabile* air sung with great expression to cornet accompaniment and epitomises English opera in Ireland throughout much of the nineteenth century. To speak of opera in Ireland during this time is to speak essentially of opera in Dublin, for there never has been an Irish National Opera, and, understandably, the principal visiting companies did not travel outside the capital except for occasional engagements in Belfast, Cork and Limerick.

As a composer, Balfe bestrode the field of English opera as much in Dublin as in London, from the production of his *Siege of Rochelle* in 1835 until the end of the century, to be followed by a second Irishman, William Vincent Wallace, still remembered for his *Maritana*. In Dublin, both received the ultimate compliment, or absurdity, by having an opera performed in Italian, Balfe: *The Bohemian Girl* in 1858, with the renowned soprano and tenor, Marietta Piccolomini and Antonio Giuglini, and Wallace in 1877 with *Maritana*.

In Dublin during the nineteenth century, of German opera sung in German there was none, but occasional invasions were made

The Gods, reminiscence of the Dublin operatic season, 1874. The Gods remained an integral part of the Dublin opera scene throughout the nineteenth century. Here they are shown lowering a dove to the prima donna amidst an avalanche of bouquets. Following the successful performance of a big aria this was the highest compliment that could be paid to her. Later, they would unharness the horses and draw her carriage back to her hotel. In return she would serenade them from her window. Since the date of the illustration is December 1874 the artist receiving the ovation is Therese Tietjens. 'White hat in the pit!' was the cry which greeted any man taking his seat there wearing a hat that was not black, and was the signal for him to be pelted with anything from paper darts to apples.

by French companies. In 1824 a group from Paris brought a number of now almost forgotten operas by Boieldieu, Isouard, Dalayrac, Devienne, Gaveaux and Audinot. In 1850 a second French company arrived via the St James's Theatre, London, with Boieldieu's *La Dame Blanche* and Auber's *Le Domino Noir, Les Diamants de la Couronne* and *Fra Diavolo*. Then, in 1870, Hortense Schneider, the most famous operetta singer of the Second Empire, arrived, just as that empire was disintegrating, with Offenbach's *La Grande Duchesse de Gerolstein, Barbe Bleue* and *Orphée aux Enfers*. Finally, in 1875, a French company revived some of the operas by Boieldieu and Auber already performed in 1850 and to these added productions of Herold's *Zampa*, Halevy's *Mousquetaires de la Reine,* Donizetti's *La Fille du Régiment* and Rossini's *Guillaume Tell*.

It was Italian opera that really established itself in the nineteenth century. Between 1810 and 1820 Mozart's operas had been introduced but without particular success. The first to reach Dublin, on 31 August 1811, was *Così fan tutte*, when Frederick Jones brought a company of Italians from the King's Theatre in the Haymarket, London, to give a short season at Crow Street. Michael Kelly, the Irish tenor, came with them as stage manager. But it was not until some twenty years later that Italian opera really began to take root. By then, travel was becoming easier, first through the steamship, later because of the railway, and so, from 1829 onwards, Italian companies coming from England began to visit Dublin at regular intervals. In the beginning, they brought with them the operas of Rossini, including *Il Barbiere di Siviglia,* later, the works of Bellini, Donizetti and some minor composers.

By 1840 Italian opera had begun to reach full flower, for in this and in succeeding years, Dublin opera-goers could hear the operas of Bellini and Donizetti sung by the greatest quartet of singers of their time, the soprano Giuditta Grisi, the tenor Giovanni Mario, the baritone Antonio Tamburini and the bass Luigi Lablache, whose mother, incidentally, is said to have been Irish. Then in 1848, Jenny Lind, the original Swedish Nightingale, arrived leading a company with Balfe as conductor and sang

*The burning of the Theatre Royal in Hawkins Street, Dublin, on
9 February 1880. The theatre was opened on 18 January 1821, having
been built on premises formerly occupied by the Royal Dublin Society to
designs by Breasley for the proprietor Henry Harris. After the closing
of the Crow Street Theatre, it became the venue for opera in Dublin.
(From the collection of F. E. Dixon in the Dublin Civic Museum)*

in *La Sonnambula, I Puritani* and *La Figlia del Reggimento,* with
phenomenal success. The next year, Catherine Hayes, the young
soprano from Limerick, having established her reputation on the
Continent and at Covent Garden, returned for her first operatic
appearances in Dublin, singing *Lucia* and *Norma*. In 1861 the
eighteen-year-old Adelina Patti, the first great singer to appear in
Dublin whose voice can still be heard on gramophone records,
arrived.

Verdi's operas had been introduced to Dublin in 1849 with a
performance in English of *Ernani*. *Il Trovatore* in Italian followed
in 1855, *La Traviata* in 1856 with Piccolomini, *Rigoletto* in 1857
with Ronconi, and *Macbeth* in 1859 with Pauline Vixardot Garcia,
who on 27 February would write to her confidant, the conductor,
Julius Rietz, 'I like Dublin very much – the audiences here are
very enthusiastic and I am a great favourite.' *Un Ballo in Maschera*
would be performed in 1861. Wagner had to wait much longer
for his works to arrive and then they were presented only in

translation. *Lohengrin* in Italian appeared in 1875 with two world-famous artists, Emma Albani and Victor Maurel, as Elsa and Telbramund. *Der Fliegende Holländer* was produced in English by the Carl Rosa Company in 1878.

But the old Theatre Royal in Hawkins Street in which these performances had taken place was burned down on 9 February 1880 and its loss would contribute to changes of fashion in the style of opera in Dublin for the remainder of the century. Italian companies still occasionally came on tour (to the Gaiety Theatre, which had opened on 27 November 1871) but this was now the era of the Carl Rosa Opera. This company had been founded to produce opera in English, and with the intention of improving standards of both repertory and performance. It had first appeared in Dublin in December 1875, at the Theatre Royal. Charles Santley and the Dublin baritone William Ludwig (Ledwidge) were among the artists. Undoubtedly it presented more uniform if less exhilarating performances. Moreover opera in the vernacular was then having a vogue. (Was this due to the enormous success of the Gilbert and Sullivan operas?) For a time, at least, the importance of the great singer in Dublin opera, like the light of other days, had faded.

Contemporary Irish Music
Colman Pearce

Strictly speaking, the subject-matter of this essay should be the music of living, or recently deceased, Irish composers. However, I think that a quick backward glance to survey some of the people and events that have led us to our present position might prove helpful.

It is demonstrably true that all those nations which have managed over a long period to withstand the yoke of oppression, have also contrived to establish a recognisable national identity in the Arts. Important 'schools' have flourished in the Netherlands, Spain, England, Austria, Germany, Italy and latterly, the United States. But, until this century, we look in vain for any Irish 'school' in any of the Arts that does not precede medieval times.

The pivotal figure in our musical renascence is Sir Charles Villiers Stanford (1852–1924). Despite the too-audible salutes to his hero Brahms, Stanford also 'worked the mines' of his native folk-music, as bequeathed to him by Bunting, Joyce, Petrie and Moore. His success as a composer in the European 'art-music' area undoubtedly acted as a stimulus to Hamilton Harty (1879–1941) and John F. Larchet (1884–1967). Both of these wrote many original works imbued with a distinctly Irish flavour, and both also made tasteful and often beautiful arrangements of Irish folk tunes, as did Herbert Hughes (1882–1937) and Charles Wood, who succeeded Stanford as professor at Cambridge. Dr Larchet, as Professor of Music in University College, Dublin, from 1921 to 1958, exerted great influence as a teacher on succeeding Irish composers. Arthur Duff (1899–1956), whose lyrical gifts owed something to the influence of Delius, has left us some superb arrangements, and, although his output of original works was small, the *Irish Suite for strings*, and *Echoes of Georgian Dublin* for orchestra, are beautifully wrought and attest to a very real creative talent.

Having adverted to the influence of Brahms and Delius, it may be the opportune time to deal, briefly, with the question of foreign influences, direct and indirect. Irish composers trying to find an individual style were open to the prevailing, not to say all-pervading, leading influences at work in Europe at the time. Without dwelling on the various 'isms' (e.g. French Impressionism), suffice to say that nearly all the Irish composers born in the first quarter of this century could acknowledge a debt to, variously, Debussy, Ravel, Stravinsky (wearing, at this time, but two hats!), Mahler, Sibelius, Prokofiev, Hindemith, *et al*. In other words, we were in exactly the same position as any other civilised European country; cross-pollination has always been a healthy and detectable activity in the Arts, not least in music. These elements, mixed with our, by now, surging nationalist strain, and aided and abetted by the English folk-song revival (ironic though that may seem!) helped forge the musical personalities of our older composers.

Mention must be made here of two English composers whose emotional bond with Ireland, and involvement with Irish culture, have made them, in the opinion of many (both in England and Ireland), 'spiritual' Irishmen. E. J. (Jack) Moeran (1894–1950) was born near London, of an Irish father and English mother. His finest works are undoubtedly his songs and appropriately enough, the *Seven Poems of James Joyce*, written in 1929, are his masterpieces. Sir Arnold Bax (1883–1953) was a high-priest of the 'Celtic twilight' movement; he was a great lover of our folklore, and was an intimate of Yeats, Lady Gregory, Padraic Colum (many of whose poems he set) and others prominent in the Irish Literary Revival. He regretted that he could find no trace of Irish ancestry in his forebears! Poetically, both he and Moeran died in Ireland.

John F. Larchet (1885–1967), pictured on his 80th birthday. Larchet succeeded Kitson as Professor of Music of the National University of Ireland (University College, Dublin) in 1920. As Professor of composition at the Royal Irish Academy of Music he was the teacher of many of the present generation of Irish composers.

Howard Ferguson, born in Belfast in 1908, was educated in London where he studied with R. O. Morris, and has lived there ever since. He wrote two violin sonatas, an *Octet* for the same players as Schubert's, a piano sonata and a *Partita* which exists in an orchestral version as well as one for two pianos. These works do not employ traditional Irish material, though Dr Ferguson has published arrangements of traditional songs and other melodies.

Aloys Fleischmann, born in Munich in 1910, was reared in Cork, where be became Professor of Music at University College in 1934. A friend of Bax, he belongs to a group of Irish composers (see below) who favour integration with the European mainstream as far as technical language is concerned. His texts, however, are invariably by Irish writers, and the titles of his orchestral and choral works indicate his deep interest in Irish subjects, which have so often been the source of his inspiration. Among his more important orchestral works are the Overture, *The Four Masters* (1948), *Clare's Dragoons* (1944) and the *Songs of Colmcille* (1964), the last two works including a mixed-voice chorus.

Frederick May (b. 1911) was a pupil of Vaughan Williams in

London, and later of Egon Wellesz in Vienna. His style is broadly European; his essentially lyrical gifts are shown to best advantage in his songs, the *String Quartet*, and in his orchestral piece *Sunlight and Shadow* (1955).

Brian Boydell (b. 1917), Professor of Music at Trinity College, Dublin, studied with Herbert Howells and Patrick Hadley in London, and with Dr Larchet in Dublin. His compositions can be loosely categorised as (a) those with an Irish flavour – viz. the *Shielmartin Suite* for orchestra and various vocal works with Irish texts, and (b) those works written in the European 'mainstream' language, which form the bulk of his output. Dr Boydell has contributed some important pieces to the orchestral repertoire, notably *In Memoriam Mahatma Gandhi* (1948), *Megalithic Ritual Dances* (1956), *Meditation and Fugue* (1956) and *Symphonic Inscapes* (1968).

In the period 1935–1950, there tended to be a sharp division between the approach of the composers just discussed, and that of the direct followers of the Stanford–Larchet line, representing a development of overtly 'Irish'-flavoured music. In this tradition we find Walter Beckett (b. 1914), T. C. Kelly (b. 1917), Daniel McNulty (b. 1920), Havelock Nelson (b. 1917), Eamon O Gallchobhair (b. 1906) and Redmond Friel (b. 1907), all of whom have enriched our musical life with some delightful, if small-scale, original works, and many valued and accomplished arrangements of our folk-tunes. Joan Trimble (b. 1915) is in the same tradition. Her opera *Blind Raftery* was commissioned by BBC Television.

A figure somewhat apart is Seán O Ríada (1931–71). A graduate in music of Cork University, he was a man of singular musicality. In the last eleven years or so of his short life, he espoused the cause of Irish traditional music and his performances in this genre with his small group of musicians were revelatory. His score for the film *Mise Eire* (1959) proved very popular, and O Ríada became something of a cult figure. His personal magnetism undoubtedly enhances his reputation as a composer, for his output was quite small. Apart from his film-scores, his main works are *Hercules Dux Ferrariae* for String Orchestra, the song-cycle *In*

Memoriam Aloys Fleischmann (Senior) and *Nomos No. 2* for baritone soloist, chorus and orchestra.

A. J. (Archie) Potter (b. 1918) studied with Vaughan Williams, and many of his works have passages which show a musical affinity with his mentor, though he possesses a strongly individual style of his own. He commands a virtuoso orchestral technique, shown to excellent advantage in his *Overture to a Kitchen Comedy* (1950), the *Concerto da Chiesa* for piano and orchestra, and the *Sinfonia De Profundis* (1968).

Gerard Victory, Director of Music at Radio Telefis Eireann since 1967, is probably the most prolific of contemporary Irish composers. He writes with mastery in a variety of idioms, from light music to avant-garde, and has a particular felicity in setting texts in many languages. Among his more important works are *Symphony No. 2* (1976), *Kriegslieder* (1967), the opera *Chatterton* (1972) and *The Poor Old Flea* (1959).

James Wilson (b. 1922 in London) has been living in Ireland since 1949. A pupil of Alec Rowley, he has a large output, the main works being *Symphony No. 1* (1967), the opera *Twelfth Night* (1968), *Tain,* a monodrama for soprano, piano and percussion (1974) and *Symphony No. 2* (1975).

John Kinsella (b. 1932) has written a good deal of chamber music, as well as two cello concertos and *Rondo* and *Montage* for orchestra. His style is loosely serial, though he does not eschew resultant tonality, as evinced in his most recent work *String Quartet No. 3* (1978).

Seoirse Bodley (b. 1933) studied in Germany with Johann David. Initially his style was influenced by Hindemith, but his abiding interest in Irish folk-music, and his awareness of the latest developments of Stockhausen, Boulez, etc., have recently led to a very interesting phase in his development of a strongly individual style. His orchestral work *A Small White Cloud Drifts Over Ireland* (1976) and the choral suite *A Chill Wind* (1978) reveal a fascinating integration of traditional Irish music elements with already skilful use of modern devices. Earlier important works include the *Symphony for Chamber Orchestra* (1964), *Meditations on Lines from Patrick Kavanagh* (1971), and *Configurations* (1967).

Bernard Geary (b. 1934) is a graduate in music of University College Cork. He has written an opera for children, *The Plaisham*; *Provocations for Strings* (1964), an *Elegy for Small Orchestra* (1977) and *Triptych for Orchestra* (1973), which features a soprano soloist and has an interesting synthesis of jazz and classical styles.

The newest generation of Irish composers includes, amongst many names of promise, the following: David Byers (b. 1947), Philip Hammond (b. 1951), Frank Corcoran (b. 1944), Roger Doyle (b. 1949), John Buckley (b. 1951), Eric Sweeney (b. 1948), John Gibson (b. 1951), Gerald Barry (b. 1952) and Raymond Deane (b. 1953). They have all shown accomplishment in various manners; their future development is awaited with interest and high hopes.

In such a short article, many names have regrettably been omitted. We are, at this time, standing very close to the picture – only the perspective of time will show the true shapes and patterns of our contemporary musical progress.

The Popular Tradition in Ireland Today
David Hammond

The island of Ireland today is vibrant with reels, jigs, hornpipes, slow airs and songs. This surge of traditional Irish music over the last twenty-five years is something of a phenomenon, something that approaches a social revolution.

Traditional music and other traditional art forms, visual and literary, have always existed if not alongside at least adjacent to what can be described as 'the classical tradition'. This classical tradition perpetuated by academics, the professions and the world of commerce, has never been totally accepted by all members of society, nor has it even been freely available. The small farmer, the landless labourer, the industrial worker, in the past excluded from education and even literacy, established their own traditions and the sum of these traditions is what we call folklore. The plural form, traditions, is an important distinction because of the wide variations from region to region.

These traditions, in the past intensely local, were products – and the best of them were splendid products – of environment and inheritance and the consequent poverty and isolation. They were the creations of an underground movement, a subterranean culture, not necessarily subversive, considered unimportant by the ruling classes.

During the twentieth century social factors have been slowly changing all this and among these education has been a profound influence. Ironically, the more developed the education the quicker are the traditions eroded; the more alive it is to the apparent needs of society the more it introduces the 'classical tradition' and eschews the culture of the kitchen and the street. Included in this educative process are, of course, the influence of churches, newspapers, magazines, more recently radio and television, and the contacts with other cultures that tourism and mobility of labour establish in one form or another. The subsoil is disturbed and the underground cultures are laid bare, stripped of intimacy, secrecy and imagination. An early sign that traditional music was losing its ambience and was blundering into the public domain was the invention of the *ceili* band where combinations of piano, drums, fiddles, piano-accordions and saxophones battered out dance tunes for several hours at a stretch. A good time was had by all but it was not very musical. It was enough to drive a number of Irish musicians in other directions, in search of the origins of the tradition.

This search was to result in a rediscovery of Irish music and was to change the shape and texture as well as the sound of Irish life. Like all discoveries, the rediscovery of traditional music in Ireland started from more than one centre – there were several near-simultaneous combustions in the late 1950s.

Seán O Ríada, an Irish composer trained in Europe and lecturing in Cork, tiring of the wan arrangements of Irish airs that paled into insignificance alongside European masterpieces, surrendered to the interior pressures of his own roots. They forced him to become himself. He chose a small number of handpicked traditional players and with inspiration, discipline and sheer musical ability they developed into the imaginative group that became known as *Ceoltoiri Chulann*.

Perhaps it is not strictly true to describe all the work of *Ceoltoiri Chulann* as traditional music. For some of O Ríada's arrangements centred on music that was classical and European in its origins. It belongs to the era of the great harpers of the eighteenth century, the society of the big houses, and *Ceoltoiri Chulann* gave it a new currency.

Around the same period four young Irishmen exiled in New York launched into their own voyage of self-discovery. The Clancy Brothers and Tommy Makem were almost certainly the first to adapt traditional Irish songs to a group and a beat. They sang their own native music with spontaneity and sympathy, with a good musical sense and with instinctive sensitivity. Their communication with an audience was magical and it depended as much on their early experience in the theatre as it did on their music.

The inevitable happened. The vision of the Clancy Brothers and Tommy Makem's conquest of America in Aran jerseys was too much for the young male population of Ireland. Mistaking the group's simplicity for a carefree amateurism and their bonhomie for a lot of impromptu wisecracks, and forgetting the legacy of music the group had nurtured before they ever went near a stage, hundreds of folk groups thronged the pubs of Ireland, driving out the morose, the companionable, setting the walls vibrating. It was a Folk Boom, commercially exploited, a far cry from the sources of the revival of Irish music and for a lot of people it was anything but pleasant. Some longed for the good old days when folk music had been old hat.

But the music proved too strong to be endangered by the mindlessness of the singing pubs. All the pioneer work of men like Seamus Ennis, Seán O Boyle, Seán MacReamóinn, Proinsias O'Conluain and Ciaran MacMathuna, who travelled throughout the 1950s to record traditional music in its own intimate environments and broadcast it with the esteem it deserved, was exerting its own influence.

The new generation of musicians maturing in the present decade had grown up amid the various confusions of the revival, the good and the bad, the faddish and the spurious. The best of them were selective, gifted and dedicated to a vision, eager for experiment and evolution but with a kinship for the past.

Donal Lunney, for instance, has formed the Bothy Band, musicians with skill, sensitive to form and to mood, adventurous in exploring the interior of the traditional modes and revealing them to audiences in Europe and America as well as in Ireland. Clannad, a family group from Donegal, are progressive in their approach to old forms, informed by good judgement and musicianship. Horslips, a Celtic rock band, witty, articulate and electrified, find contemporary relevance in ancient Irish myths.

The Chieftains play on the vast stage of the world, enshrining in their music the grace and the greatness of Seán O Ríada, without whom it might never have happened.

Then there are the solo performers – fiddlers like John Doherty from Donegal, singers like Geordie Hanna from Tyrone, who were there before the revival and whom the revival has not neglected. And there are younger men like Paul Brady, singer and instrumentalist, unique in his talent, his own musical man.

In whole areas of the country, places like Clare, parts of Wexford, Galway, Kerry, traditional music is still endemic in the population, restored and enriched by the peripheries of Dublin, Belfast and the *Fleadh Ceóil*.

The acceptance of traditional music into the public domain owes much to the organisational groundwork of bodies like Gael-Linn and Comhaltas Ceoltoiri Eireann. There are dangers in the acceptance; regional and individual styles may be blurred, for instance, and repertoires made uniform.

But there are healthy signs. For one thing, there is a recognition of the music as a relevant art form, open to a wide range of critical sensibilities, providing opportunities for challenges and the sharing of new techniques. For another, the music is rescued from the attention of well-meaning pedants, nativists and primitivists, releasing it from the reservation of being merely 'an Irish heritage' or the symbol of 'an Irish Ireland', into the wide world to take its chance with other music.

Music in Ireland – the Future
Anthony Hughes

Any attempt to forecast the future development of music in Ireland would have to take cognisance of the remarkable transformation our musical life has experienced in the past thirty years. Michael Bowles' initiative provided the nucleus of an orchestra, which in spite of many objections, recruited foreign musicians in post-war years as it expanded. We find it now as the RTE Symphony Orchestra embarking on foriegn tours, its public concerts in Dublin, repeated in Cork and Limerick given to full houses. The RTE Concert Orchestra tours centres which have not a suitable auditorium for the full Symphony Orchestra. Recently the BBC has enlarged its Northern Ireland Orchestra. One hopes for the establishment of an orchestra in Cork, and frequent exchanges of concerts.

The New Irish Chamber Orchestra, many of whose players are in the RTESO, explore a repertory similar to the Ulster Orchestra, travels extensively to towns which otherwise would never have a professional concert, and provides a platform for young soloists. NICO has travelled abroad, gathering golden opinions, and is soon to tour the USA and the USSR. This momentum will gather pace.

The lack of a Concert Hall in Dublin is a shameful blight on a European capital city. The Great Hall of UCD in Earlsfort Terrace, currently being adapted to provide a studio auditorium of some 1200 seats, will give the RTESO a desirable home, but its restricted seating capacity precludes its use for visiting International orchestras. The much publicised Kennedy Hall designed by the late Raymond McGrath would have been, and still could be, one of Europe's most beautiful and exciting concert venues. A new-found political maturity stimulated by the emergent European Parliament, with the possible boost of an oil-well, may yet allow its construction and place Dublin on the international concert circuit.

Dublin now has three amateur or training orchestras, and a Baroque orchestra, Cork a semi-professional symphony orchestra and a youth orchestra. Belfast too has its amateur youth orchestra. The most encouraging phenomenon of the 1970s has been the emergence of the Irish National Youth Orchestra. Within a decade it has doubled its size, and there is now the keenest competition for every place. The heartening prospect emerges that henceforth we shall have a steady stream of musicians to fill vacancies arising in Dublin and Belfast, and perhaps new orchestras in Cork, Limerick, Galway and Derry, which might pair occasionally for large-scale works.

The Department of Education in the Republic has in recent years concentrated on expanding school programmes to develop an intelligent listening public. It is open to criticism that it has not provided instruments for ensemble or individual music-making, as is the practice in Northern Ireland. Newer schools have music wings and audio-visual equipment, but music rooms, in fact, have in some cases been assigned to other subjects. A very few boys' schools have fine orchestras or brass bands, but it is regrettable that so many boys at second level receive no musical education whatever. The Arts Council, in awarding scholarships to young musicians for advanced study, has stepped in to highlight a serious defect in educational policy at official level. Irish students have benefited from scholarships awarded by Austrian, French, German, Italian and Netherlands Governments. Cultural agreements could build on this foundation, and bring many foreign students to Ireland in other disciplines in which our higher institutions excel. A case must be made for funds to be made available from Local Government sources to support outstanding young students at our Academies and Music Schools. A most\progressive school in Mullingar reserves 16 free places for musically gifted boys, who receive a commendably broad musical training in addition to their general education. These young men, now at University level, are likely to make a positive contribution to musical life outside our cities.

The thinly spread population of our western seaboard must receive special attention since teachers are now reluctant to live in country areas. New technology with video cassettes and closed circuit televisual booths can do much to transform class teaching for more isolated schools.

Short Opera seasons in Wexford, Dublin, Cork and Belfast depend on immense voluntary work and on the continuity of support from private firms to supplement Arts Council grants. The rebuilding of the Belfast Opera House is a most encouraging portent. The closure of the Gaiety Theatre in Dublin or the Cork Opera House, sometimes surreptitiously hinted, must be resisted at all costs. Performances with piano or small orchestral resources such as those given by the Irish National Opera or the Northern Studio Opera, will remain most valuable in smaller centres as a foundation for promoting future audiences.

The successful organisation of Dublin Twentieth-Century Music Festivals has proved to visitors that Irish composers are aware of contemporary international trends; some have attained notable success at the International Rostrum in Paris. Among the younger figures, Barry, Buckley, Deane, with the somewhat older Bodley and Kinsella, will come more into prominence and enhance the achievements of Boydell, Fleischmann, Potter and Victory. The absence of an Irish publishing house has hindered the dissemination of our music. RTE has for some years past purchased the scores and rights of every viable work by an Irish composer and given it at least one hearing. The scores and copies of parts are available to external organisations. This praiseworthy initiative deserves wider recognition and ought to receive a sustained promotional campaign abroad.

This year Queen's University, Belfast, in conjunction with the Arts Council of Northern Ireland, has appointed a Composer in Residence. This should prove a great stimulus both to students at the University and to the musical life of the whole province.

Until recently our finest musicians have left Ireland to pursue their careers, That it is now possible to win international acclaim, and reside in Ireland has been proved possible by such artists as Bernadette Greevy (contralto), Geraldine O'Grady (violin), John O'Conor (piano), Desmond Hunter and Gerard Gillen (organ). Their living presence in the community encourages and inspires younger aspirants.

Plans have been laid for a music archive, and a comprehensive music library for the eighties. A rising group of scholars will surely focus their attention on aspects of our history, and examine the notational, linguistic and instrumental aspects of Irish folk music, sifting the intrusions of recent commercialism, and relate their findings to similar studies of other cultures. The possibilities are exciting and attainable. It is irrational to withhold the necessary resources.

Selected Bibliography
(With editorial comments)

No comprehensive history of Irish music, or of musical activity in Ireland, which contains reliable information has yet been published, although certain special areas have been adequately covered. *The New History of Ireland*, which is in the process of being published, will contain contributions on Music and Society in Ireland by Professor Boydell (up to 1850) and Professor Fleischmann (1850–1921), and the forthcoming sixth edition of *Grove's Dictionary of Music and Musicians* will contain articles incorporating recent research concerning Irish composers, musical personalities and other aspects of musical life in Ireland.

GENERAL INFORMATION

Acton, Charles, *Irish Music and Musicians* (Irish Heritage Series, No. 15, Dublin 1978)

Fleischmann, Aloys (ed.), *Music in Ireland: A Symposium* (Cork 1952)

Flood, W. G. Grattan, *A History of Irish Music* (Dublin 1905) (Reprinted, Irish University Press 1970)
A fairly comprehensive and oft-quoted book which is unfortunately very unreliable.

Groocock, J., *A General Survey of Music in the Republic of Ireland* (Dublin 1961)

Meally, Victor (ed.), *Encyclopaedia of Ireland* (Dublin 1968)
Containing the following articles on music:
Boydell, Brian: General Historical Survey
Breathnach, Breandan: Traditional Music and Irish Dancing

Hughes, Anthony: Professional Music
Fleischmann, Aloys: Amateur Music, Musical Education
Ross, Rev. Canon Robert: Church Music
Sennett, Graham: Pop Music and Ballads

OPERA AND THEATRE MUSIC

(The first two books evoke the atmosphere of their subjects very
well, but many factual details have been proved incorrect. They
should therefore be treated with caution.)

Kelly, Michael, *Reminiscences* (London 1826, 2 vols) (Reprinted
under the title *Solo Recital*, London 1972)

O'Keeffe, John, *Recollections of the Life of John O'Keeffe Written by
Himself* (London 1826, 2 vols)

Sheldon, Esther K., *Thomas Sheridan of Smock Alley* (Princeton
1967)

Stockwell, La Tourette, *Dublin Theatres and Theatre Customs*
(Kingsport, Tennessee 1938)

Walsh, T. J., *Opera in Dublin 1705–1797* (Dublin 1973)

OTHER SPECIAL SUBJECTS AND PERIODS

Boydell, Brian, *Venues for Music in 18th century Dublin*. Dublin
Historical Record December 1975

Delany, Mary Granville, *The Autobiography and Correspondence of
Mary Granville, Mrs. Delany*. Ed. Lady Llanover (London 1861,
3 vols.)
This valuable source of references to life in eighteenth-century
Dublin contains numerous episodes concerning music.

Fleischmann, A. and Gleeson, R., 'Music in Ancient Munster and
Monastic Cork'. In *Journal of the Cork Historical and Archaeo-
logical Society*, Vol. LXX 1965

Harrison, Frank Ll, *Music in Medieval Britain* (London 1958) contains interesting references to early church music in Ireland

Hogan, Ita M., *Anglo-Irish Music 1780–1830* (Cork 1966)

O'Sullivan, Donal, *Carolan* (London 1958, 2 vols)

Piggott, Patrick, *The Life and Music of John Field* (London 1973)

Rimmer, Joan, *The Irish Harp* (Cork 1969)

Townsend, Horatio, *Handel's visit to Dublin* (Dublin 1852)

TRADITIONAL MUSIC

Breathnach, An t-Athair Pól, *Ar gCeol Féinig* (Dublin 1920); *Ceol ár Sinsear* (Dublin)

Breathnach, Breandan, *Folk Music and Dances of Ireland*, Educational Company (Dublin 1971)

Bunting, Edward, *Ancient Irish Music*, 3 vols, Reprinted (Dublin 1967)

Ceol, *Journal of Irish Music*, in progress (Dublin)

Corkery, Daniel, *The Hidden Ireland* (Dublin 1967)

Costella, E. (Mrs), *Amhrain Mhuighe Seola* (Dublin 1920)

Clandillon, *Londubh an Chairn*, 3 vols (O.U.P. 1927)

Freeman, M., *Songs from Ballyrowney*, Journal of FSS, Vol. VI

Hardebeck, C. G., *Seoda Ceoil,* 3 vols., Pigott (Dublin 1908)

Heneby, Richard, *Handbook of Irish Music* (Cork U.P. 1928)

Hughes, Herbert, *Irish Country Songs,* 4 vols, Boosey (London 1909–36)

Joyce, P. W., *Old Irish Folk Music and Song* (Dublin 1909); *Ancient Music of Ireland* (Dublin 1912)

Kennedy, Peter, *Folk Songs of Britain and Ireland*, Cassell (London 1975)

O Baoighill S., *Cnuasacht de Cheoltai Uldah* (Belfast 1944)

O Baoill, C. (ed.) *Amhrain Chuige Uldah*, Gilbert Dalton (Dublin 1976)

O Baoill, S. M., *Ceolta Gael,* Mercier Press (Cork 1975)

O Boyle, Seán, *The Irish Song Tradition*, Gilbert Dalton (Dublin 1976)

O Canainn, Tomas, *Traditional Music in Ireland* (London 1978)

O'Keefe, *Handbook of Irish Dances* (Dublin 1954)

O Lochlainn, *Irish Street Ballads*, Three Candles Press (Dublin 1939); *More Irish Street Ballads* (Dublin 1965)

O'Neill, Francis, *The Music of Ireland*, Republished N.Y. (1964); *The Dance Music of Ireland*, Republished (Dublin 1969)

O'Sullivan, Donal, *Irish Folk Music and Song* (Dublin 1961); *Songs of the Irish* (Dublin 1967)

O Tuama, Sean Og., *An Choisir Cheoil,* i–xii (Dublin)

Petrie, George, *Ancient Music of Ireland*, Farnborrough (1968);
The Complete Collection of Irish Music as noted by George Petrie
ed. (Stanford, 1902–05)

Zimmerman, G. D., *Irish Political Street Ballads and Rebel Songs,
1780–1900*, La Sirène (Geneva, Switzerland 1966)

Discography

IRISH TRADITIONAL MUSIC

Claddagh Records, Dublin:
Deora Aille, Máire Aine Ní Dhonncha   CC6
An Áill Bhan, Sean 'ac Donncha   CC9

Gael-Linn, Dublin:
Rann na Reivste Ceol agus Amhráin   CEF 036
Máire Ní Scolai, Songs in Irish   CEF 029
Seán O Ríada, Instrumental and Vocal   CEF 032

Mulligan Recordings, Dublin:
Andy Irvine and Paul Brady, Songs and Airs   LUN 008
Songs of Ulster

Polydor, London:
Planxty, Songs and Airs   2783 186

Transatlantic Records, London:
The Dubliners with Luke Kelly   TRA 116

Topic, London:
Grand Airs from Connemara   12 T 177
More Grand Airs from Connemara   12 T 202
Also: Recordings of Paddy Tunney,
Robert Cinnamond and Sarah Makem

Ulster Folk Museum, Co. Down:
Adam in Paradise: The Songs of Eddie Butcher
Ulster's Flowery Vale: Songs from Various Singers

All the above records are commercial recordings.
Private collections in BBC Recorded Programmes
Library and in Folk Music Department, University
College, Dublin.

THE POPULAR TRADITION

1. 'Ulster's Flowery Vale'   BBC Radio Enterprises
   A sampler of Ulster traditional music   REC 28M
2. 'Out of the wind, into the sun'   Mulligan LUN 013
   The Bothy Band
3. 'John Doherty'   Gael-Linn
   Donegal fiddler
4. 'Lough Erne Shore'   Sruthán/Mulligan LUNA 334
   Songs by Paddy Tunney
5. The Chieftains   Claddagh
   No. 1   CC2
   No. 2   CC7
   No. 3   CC10
   No. 4   CC14
6. 'O Ríada's Farewell'   Claddagh CC12
7. 'Mrs Sarah Makem'   Topic 12 T 182
   Ulster Ballad singer
8. 'Welcome here, kind stranger'   Mulligan LUN 024
   Singer: Paul Brady
9. 'Dúlamán'   Gael-Linn CEF 058
   Clannad
10. 'The Book of Invasions'   Horslips MOO12P
    A Celtic Symphony
11. 'Willie Clancy: The Minstrel from Clare'   Topic 12 T 175
    Uileann Piper
12. na Filí 3   Outlet SOLP 1017
13. Seosamh Ó hÉanaí   Gael-Linn CEF028
    Sean-nos singer
14. Joe Burke   Shaskeen OS361
    Accordion
15. Tony MacMahon   Gael-Linn CEF033
    Accordion

Seoirse Bodley

String Quartet	RTE St. Qt.	NIRC NIR 006
		(New Irish Recording Co.)
Prelude, Toccata and Epilogue	Charles Lynch	NIRC IFD001
Three Satires (Tri Aortha)	RTES	NIRC NIR007
Music for Strings	RTESO	Decca (USA) DL9843
I Will Walk with my Love	Culwick C.S., Dublin	NIRC DEB002

Brian Boydell

Megalithic Ritual Dances	RESO	Decca (USA) DL9843
String Quartet No. 1	Benthien Str. Qt.	RE (Deutsche Gram) 32291
String Quartet No. 2	RTE Str. Qt.	NIRC NIR006
Three Madrigals	RTES	NIRC NIR007
Dance for an Ancient Ritual ⎱	Charles Lynch	NIRC IFD 001
Capriccio ⎰		
Symphonic Inscapes	RTESO	NIRC NIR011

Edgar M. Deale
Follow Me up to Carlow — Culwick C.S. and Gillian Smith — NIRC DEB002
Down by the Salley Gardens — do. — do.
Oft in the Stilly Night — do. — do.
Choral Suite:
Pádraic Colum—Four Facets — Culwick C.S. and Hans Kohlmann, picc. — do.

Aloys Fleischmann
Suite for Piano — Charles Lynch — NIRC NIR001

T. C. Kelly
The Rakes of Mallow — Culwick C.S. — NIRC DEB002

John Kinsella
String Quartet No. 2 — RTE St. Qrt. — NIRC NIR002

John F. Larchet
Pádraic the Fiddiler — John McCormack and Fritz Kreisler — HMV DA636
At the Mid-Hour of Night — Culwick C.S. — Columbia DB585
The Dirge of Ossian / MacAnanty's Reel — RESO — DECCA DL9844
The Bard of Armagh — W. F. Watt — Columbia 4157
do. — Hubert Valentine — HMV IP324
Diarmuid's Lament — Michael O'Higgins — HMV IM358

Elizabeth Maconchy
String Quartet No. 5 — Allegri St. Qt. — ARGO SRG329
String Quartet No. 9 — Allegri St. Qt. — ARGO ZRG672
Overture – Proud Thames — LPO — Lyrita SRCS57
Ariadne — English Chamber Orch. and Heather Harper — L'oiseau Lyre (Decca) SOL331
Three Bagatelles for Oboe and Harpsichord — E. Barbirolli & V. Aveling — EMI HQS1298
Carol, Nowell — King's Coll. Choir, Cambridge — EMI ALP2290
Twelfth Night Song — Scottish Festival Chorus — EMI CLP3598

Fred May
String Quartet — Aeolian St. Qt. — Claddagh CSM2

Éamonn O'Gallagher
Báidín Fhéilimidh — Little Gaelic Singers — Decca 46031
An Sean Duine — RTES
Óró mo Churaichín — — Gael-Linn GL18
Crúibíní Muice / Tighe Cuain — RTES — Harmonica Mundi HMS30691

Seán O Ríada
Mise Éire — RTESO — Gael-Linn CEF002
Saoirse — do. — do. GL1
An Tine Bheo — do. — do. GL12
Ceol Na Laoi — do. — do. GL14
Reacaireacht an Riadaigh — Ceoltóirí Chualann — do. CEF 010
The Playboy of the Western World — do. — do. CEF 012
Ceol Na nUasal — do. — do. CEF 015
Ding Dong — do. — do. CEF 0016
O Ríada Sa Gaiety — do. — do. CEF 032
An Poc Ar Buile — do. — do. GL2
Neillí — do. — do. GL3
Mo Chailín Bán, etc. — do. — do. GL5
Vertical Man: Nomos No. 1 / Ten Poems / Three Songs by Thomas Kinsella — Bernadette Greevy & Veronica McSweeney — Claddagh CSM1
O Ríada's Farewell — S. O Ríada, harpsichord — do. CC12
The Battle of Aughrim — Ceoltóirí Chualann — do. CCT7
O Ríada's Mass — Tallaght Priory Choir — Gael-Linn CB3

A. J. Potter

Variations on a Popular Tune	RESO	Decca (USA) DL9844
Fantasia Éireannach	RELO	Gael-Linn CEF019
Celtic Songs	Veronica Dunn & Havelock Helson	EMI CLP1906
Finnegans Wake	Irish National Orch. and Choir	EMI STAL6025
Finnegans Wake	Band of the Irish Army	EMI TWO376
The Epigrams of Hilaire Belloc	RTES	NIRC NIR007
Irish Airs	RTELO	Gael-Linn CEF034
Irish Radio Favourites	RTELO	EMI MFP50026
Epigram on a Sleeping Friend	Culwick C.S.	NIRC DEB002

Charles Villiers Stanford

Irish Rhapsody No. 1		
Overture: Shamus O'Brien		GEM 123

Eric Sweeney

Gloria	Culwick C.S.	NIRC DEB002

Gerard Victory

Miroirs	NICO	NIRC NIR004
String Quartet	RTE Str. Qt.	NIRC NIR002
The Dreaming of the Bones ⎫		
Resurrection ⎬	Special Ensemble	ARGO PLP1091
The Cat and the Moon ⎭		
The Hawk's Well		
Prelude and Toccata	Charles Lynch	NIRC NIR001
Gaelic March ⎫		
Postman's Knock ⎪		
Balladeer ⎬	Special Ensemble	Ember ERL3319
Valse Aigrette ⎭		

James Wilson

Thermagistris	Charles Lynch	NIRC IFD001